SPOT

NATURE

T0015921

IN THE SWAMP

by Alissa Thielges

amicus
LEARNING

tree

egret

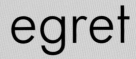

Look for these words and pictures as you read.

crayfish

alligator

This place is wet.
Many plants grow here.
It is a swamp.

Swamp water is muddy.
It is hard to see the bottom.

tree

Do you see the tree?

It is big at the bottom.

The roots start above the ground.

crayfish

Do you see the crayfish?

It digs into the mud.

It eats bugs and snails.

egret

Do you see the egret?
This bird has long legs.
It eats fish.

alligator

Do you see the alligator?

It is a big hunter.

Snap! It grabs a bird.

A river otter swims to find food.
The swamp is home
to many animals.

tree

egret

Did you find?

crayfish

alligator

SPOT

Spot is published by Amicus Learning, an imprint of Amicus
P.O. Box 227, Mankato, MN 56002
www.amicuspublishing.us

Library of Congress Cataloging-in-Publication Data
Names: Thielges, Alissa, 1995- author.
Title: In the swamp / by Alissa Thielges.
Description: Mankato, MN : Amicus Learning, an imprint of
    Amicus, 2024. | Series: Spot nature | Audience: Ages
    4–7 | Audience: Grades K–1 | Summary: "A search-
    and-find book about swamps reinforces new vocabulary
    to build reading success while close-up images captivate
    young audiences. A great early STEM book to inspire
    learning about biomes for kindergartners and first
    graders"—Provided by publisher.
Identifiers: LCCN 2023011661 (print) | LCCN 2023011662
    (ebook) | ISBN 9781645496489 (library binding) | ISBN
    9781681529370 (paperback) | ISBN 9781645496748 (pdf)
Subjects: LCSH: Swamp ecology—Juvenile literature. |
    Swamp animals—Juvenile literature. | Swamp plants—
    Juvenile literature.
Classification: LCC QH541.5.S9 T45 2024 (print) | LCC
    QH541.5.S9 (ebook) | DDC 577.68--dc23/
    eng/20230425
LC record available at https://lccn.loc.gov/2023011661
LC ebook record available at https://lccn.loc.gov/2023011662

Printed in China

Rebecca Glaser, editor
Deb Miner, series designer
Mary Herrmann, book designer
Omay Ayres, photo researcher

Photos by Dreamstime/Hakoar, 12–13,
Paul Wolf, 6–7; Getty/Istvan Kadar
Photography, cover, 16; iStock/
fusaromike, 8–9, JasonDoiy, 14–15, John
Twynam, 3, kynny, 10–11; Shutterstock/
Eric Isselee, 1, Shutterstock/
stockphotofan1, 4–5

IN THE SWAMP